Smokey Shares His Spark!

Ann Melim

Illustrated by
Ben McGuire

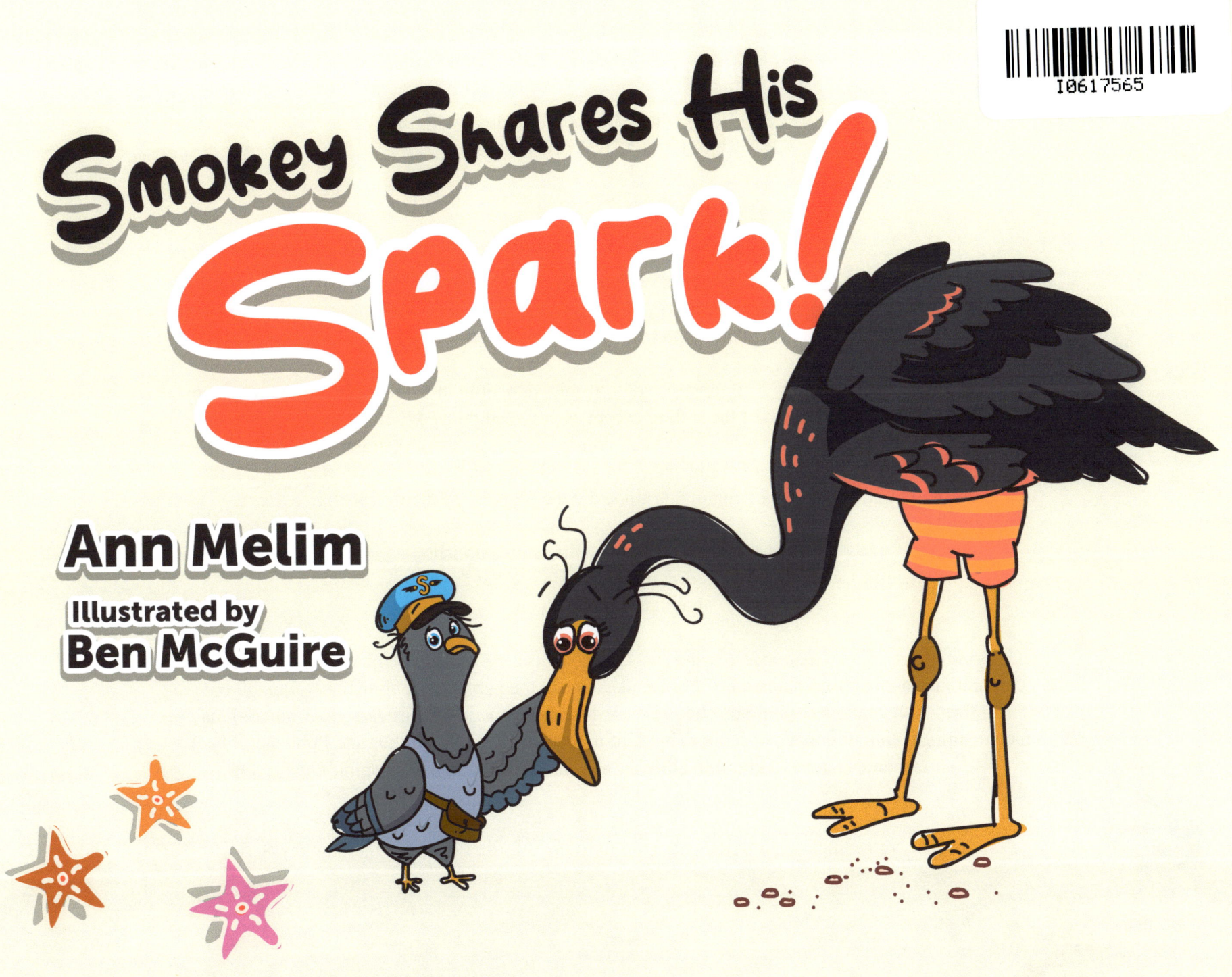

Did you know?

According to researchers, there exists only one **black flamingo** in the world. Perhaps this is his story.

for Aunt J.

To the moon and forever
In a space with no time.
Where clocks have no hands
And love speaks in rhyme.

Where roads have no ending
Above, only sapphire skies
Birds sing their own melodies
As they watch the sunrise.

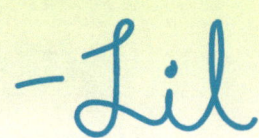

−Lil

4

for Amber and Connor.

I know I'm so lucky,
two kids beautiful and smart.
The world at your door,
go show them your spark.

-Ben

Early one morning,
before the rooster could crow,
Miss Mal woke Smokey,
real gentle and slow.

She spoke in a whisper
so no one would hear

her tell Smokey his task,
while shedding a tear:

"You found your spark here at the farm,
but it's not where your story ends.

Now it's time to share your spark,
travel more, and make new friends."

"You are kind and gentle,
thoughtful and smart.

Everyone will love you,
right from the start."

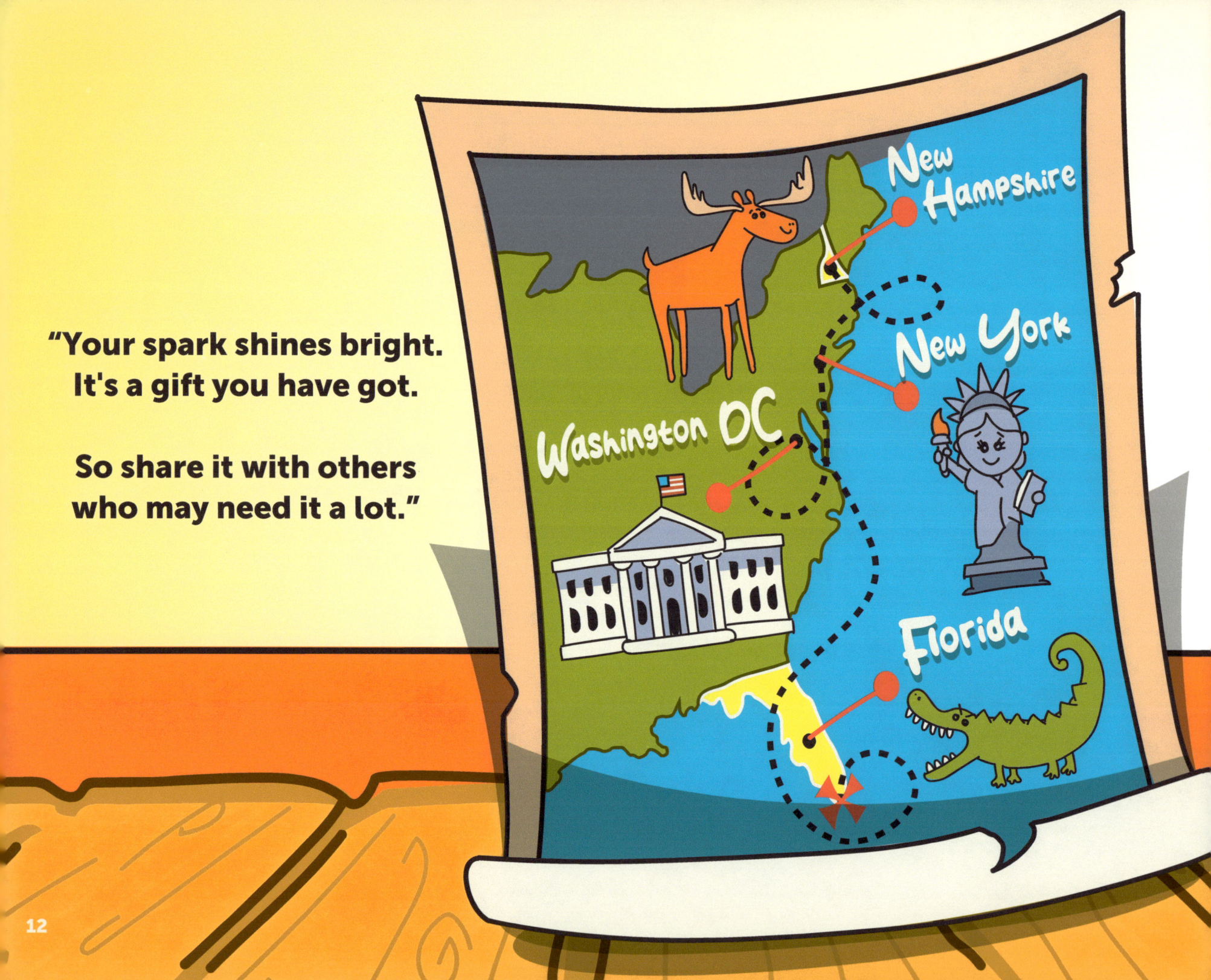

"Your spark shines bright.
It's a gift you have got.

So share it with others
who may need it a lot."

Hello from New Hampshire.
I hope you are well.

This is my pigeon
and soon you will tell

that he has a spark
so special and bright,

which he'll kindly share
with all of his might.

Miss Mal gave him a kiss,
a map and his **tote**

to carry his lunch,
a drink and a note.

Smokey then asked,
"But how will I know who this message is for?"

Miss Mal smiled and said,
"Because you'll **adore**

that she is so different and,
like you, beautifully **unique**.

She's in need of some love,
so a friend she does **seek**."

Smokey gathered his cap
and off he did fly

16

As Miss Mal waved gently,
still stars in the sky.

17

Smokey flew over **skyscrapers** and statues in the afternoon heat,

18

over big lakes and rivers,
fields of wild flowers and wheat.

He looked at his map
and to him it seemed clear

that his destination was close
and his new friend was near.

So he swooped down below
to meet his new mate.

He had reached his destination:
the Sunshiny State.

Smokey knew in an instant
the bird who needed him most.

She was easy to spot
from the Florida coast.

24

In a sea of pink flamingos,
one stood off to the side.

Her neck hung low.
She was trying to hide.

25

Smokey landed beside her
and right off the bat

he said,
"My name is Smokey,"
then took off his hat.

"I saw you from above
and your feathers of black-

you're one in a million,
but it's **spark** that you lack."

Smokey said, "I'll share my bright spark
so you can be proud

to lift your head high
in this great big pink crowd."

You are brave and gentle,
thoughtful and kind.

You listen so closely
to all creatures you find.

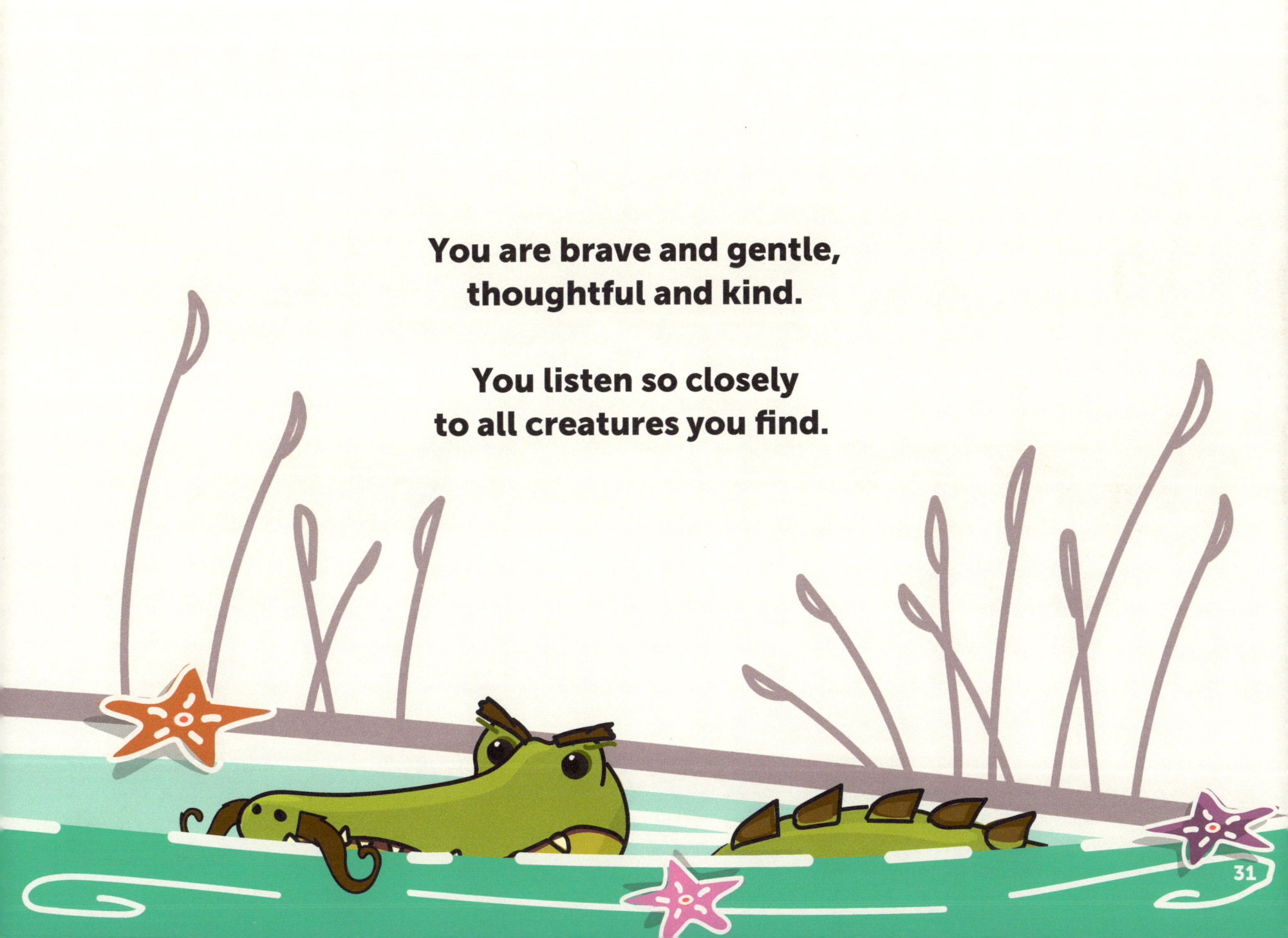

There is no need to
hang your head in **shame**.

Be proud of who you are, Peppa!
Be proud of your name!

Four pink flamingos:
Karen and Ken, Felicia and Frankie

just listened to Smokey
looking mean and so cranky.

Then all the pink flamingos laughed
and their leader just stared

at poor lonely Peppa,
until Smokey shared,

"You all may not know,
but Peppa is special inside!

I shared with her my spark,
my courage, my **pride**.

So now she can guide you
in the darkness of night

to keep you safe from the alligators
using her spark as a light.

38

She'll light the way through the **Everglades** and down to the **Keys**,

across bright blue oceans, above **canopies** of trees.

And Peppa will
lead you to safety
and find places to sleep.

She'll help you catch shrimp
and small fish by the heap.

Peppa, you've always been special
and now you should know

all it takes is a friendship
to help find your glow.

And if you ever start feeling
like you're all alone

you can find our close friendship
inside of this stone.

Thank you, my friend,
for this most precious rock.

I will always keep it close
while guiding my **FLOCK**.

My job here is done.
I'm just passing through.

I've shared my spark proudly
and now you'll share yours too!"

Glossary

Tote — Bag

Adore — Love or care for

Unique — One of a kind and special

Seek — To look for

Skyscrapers — Tall buildings

Shame — Embarrassed or upset with yourself

Pride — To be proud

Everglades — Swampy land that is covered in water and tall grass

Keys — A set of small sandy islands in southern Florida

Canopies — The tops of trees that form a ceiling or umbrella over the forest

Flock — A group of birds

About the *Author*

Ann Melim is a former high school English teacher turned dog walker extraordinaire. When she's not walking her favorite dog friends, she loves to read memoirs with her book club friends and listen to music with her husband, Joe.

With the encouragement of her high school friend, Ben McGuire, and her husband, Ann had been able to fulfill her dream of creating stories for audiences of all ages that promote friendship, courage, compassion and perseverance.

Ann lives in New Hampshire with her husband, daughter, and three rescue dogs: Atticus, Elliot and Charlotte and two cats, Tuckerman and Lola. Special thanks to Jackie Blake for helping with this project.♡

Photo of Ann and Pepper, the pup whose name inspired the main character, Peppa. (photo credit: Shannon Zurawski)

About the *Illustrator*

I told you about my family and my dog and the evil cat overlords who run my house in our first book. I told you about my hobbies like pickleball and karaoke too.

I think this time I'd just like to say…
Be kind to each other. Be kind to yourself.
Find joy in the little things.
Heck, find joy in the big things too.

Thank you to all of our readers. I hope you enjoy Smokey's adventures. It's such a pleasure to bring Ann's stories to life.

Thank you Ann for this wonderful opportunity. I'm proud of what we've created together.

How many yellow chicks are there on pages 14-15?

How is Smokey different from the other chicks?
How is he the same?

How is Peppa different from the other flamingos?
How is she the same?

Bigwig's name appears on two pages. Can you find them?
How many starfish can you find?

Where do you think Smokey will go next?
Who will he meet?

Smokey and Peppa are one-of-a-kind, unique.
What makes you special and unique?

Do you think Peppa is happy at the end of the book?
How do you know?